MEASURED BY STONE

SAM HAMILL

Curbstone Press

First Edition: 2007
Copyright © 2007 by Sam Hamill
ALL RIGHTS RESERVED

printed in the U.S. on acid-free paper
cover design: Susan Shapiro
Cover photo by F. Staud/www.phototravels.net

This book was published with the support of
the Connecticut Commission on Culture and
Tourism, the Connecticut State Legislature
through the Office of Policy & Management,
the National Endowment for the Arts, and
donations from many individuals.

Library of Congress Cataloging-in-Publication Data

Hamill, Sam.
  Measured by stone / by Sam Hamill. -- 1st ed.
     p. cm.
  ISBN 978-1-931896-40-5 (pbk. : acid-free paper)
  I. Title.

PS3558.A4235M43 2007
811'.54--dc22

                              2007021719

published by
CURBSTONE PRESS 321 Jackson St. Willimantic, CT 06226
    phone: 860-423-5110   e-mail: info@curbstone.org
                 www.curbstone.org

Acknowledgments

Ars Poetica: *Ward 6 Review*, 2006
Eyes Wide Open: *Rattle*, 2005
America, Mon Amour: *Rattle* #22, 2005
Arguing With Milosz in Vilnius: *Ploughshares*, 2005; *Best American Spiritual Writing,* 2006
On the Death of James Oscco Annamaría: *Oregon Literary Review,* 2007
Testament of the Thief: *The Progressive*, 2005
Nine Gates: *Origin*, 2007
Gazing Down the Fairway, I Think of Po Chu-i: *Drunken Boat,* 2004
To Doris Thurston on Her Eightieth Birthday: *Art Access*, 2004
On the Third Anniversary of the Ongoing War In Iraq: *The Progressive*, 2006
Cairo Qasidah: *Rattle*, 2007

A number of these poems have been translated into Spanish by Esteban Moore and included in *Ojos Bien Abiertos y Otros Poemas* (University of Carabobo, Valencia, Venezuela, 2006).

Many of these poems have also been translated into Japanese by Yusuke Keida; into Arabic by Amal Gamal; into Farsi by Farideh Hasanzadeh; and into Italian by Arturo Zilli and Alessandro Agostinelli.

To Esteban and Patricia Moore
To Yusuke Keida
And to Gray Foster and Eron Hamill

Good done to a man of character—
Letters etched in stone.

> Good done

To a man who lacks ethics and love—
Letters traced upon water.

*

Does he who gives life before he gives honor
Bow when he sees his enemies?

> Beneath a heavy load

A stone pillar may break, but tell me,
Does it buckle? Does it bend?

> —Avvaiyar (12th century)
> translated from Tamil by Thomas H. Pruiksma

CONTENTS

MEASURED BY STONE

ONE: EYES WIDE OPEN

Ars Poetica

Achilles, long after Troy,
       ventured forth again,
and in the going out,
returned home to homelessness.

And what could he know, but like Odysseus
slap of wave on bow
       and the stories they tell
about the dear dance of Thanatos and Eros

and the loves,
triumphs and betrayals of ordinary men...

Odysseus, homeless on the wine-dark sea,
       with aching heart
dreams of his Penelope
       as he sails into infinity.

Heroes are the ones
       move forward in the dark,
Seferis said as he groped on,
neither Thetis nor Circe enticing him,

but the slap of wave on shore,
scorching Mediterranean sun
       "riveted" to a rose,
and the voices,
always all those many voices in a poet's ear,

begging him to pause
       during war
to observe the certain sway
of a tall palm tree,

a sleepy Arab garden in the harsh sunlight

recalling the house that once was ours,
that was, for a moment,
       a kind of Paradise.

But dreams can sour. And wars don't simply arise.
Paradis ne pas,
       but is within,
waiting to be found
       beyond the pain,
the suffering
       to which we are not bound,
but to which we so tenaciously cling.

Paradise, Old Tom, the
       Oirish revolutionary,
liked to say,
is a sometime thing.

And Elytis, that grand land-bound sailor
of dreams, reminds: Heaven and Hell
are made of the exact same things—

confirming Lao Tzu: Success and failure
each is mother of the other.

Heraclitus: The way up is the way down.

The sea retreats; the sea swells.
We need the story that only
the going-forth can tell.
     We need the tale
that spins the spell that gives us
eyes to see.

Thus, we grope, talking to ourselves,
     unable to find
meaning in a growing darkness
wherein no meaning lies.

The heart sees far beyond the eyes.
This is no country for this old man.
I'll not find Byzantium.

My friend Ransom, no man's
idea of a pacifist,
     but a medic,
a humanist nonetheless,
     gets it exactly right:
Peace is *not* idle inaction, but
a constantly negotiated
     activity—
in the home or between nations.

I negotiate this poem with my Muse.
How could it be otherwise?
Some build prisons, some
     write prisons,
and call them sanctuaries.

Between Eros and Thanatos,
a moment of enlightenment,
          moment of bliss
amidst the redundant thunder of unholy Ares.

Thus the oarsmen sing
against the pull of oar in water,
backs bent to the rhythm
as sails unfurl the song.

In the poem of our lives,
there are many masters,
          many tongues.
The seas are mysterious, deep and wide.

We listen to the rattle of the riggings
sailing on, on,
          hungry and homeless,
sailing toward oblivion,

talking to ourselves
          as if it mattered,
eyes fixed
on the rising smoke of precisely what
horizon?

Achilles with his bloody hands and aching heel,
Odysseus with his ears on fire,
Dante emerging from the bowels of Hell...
eyes peeled

skyward...

       each with his heroic dream of Justice,
a dream of Paradise...

It is the dream itself, the listening,
       the going-forth, singing,
that keeps us all alive.

We go down to the sea and set sail
for a world beyond war,
       knowing
we will never find it.
       We are not heroes.
We sail the *Justice* and the *Mercy*
because these boats need rowing.

And when our boats go down—
as, surely, all boats must drown—
we will not
       walk upon the water
into the open arms of the Eternal Mother/Lover,

she whom we idealize
       in our robes of need
as the mind turns and the heart bleeds...

No. Not for us, salvation.
Sustained by a few essential metaphors—
       the tale, the telling,
the mind's music, the heart's vision...

we venture out, each alone, to find
that the going-forth is home.

Eyes Wide Open

The little olive-skinned girl
        peered up at me
from the photograph

with her eyes wide open,

deep brown beautiful eyes
        that bore silent witness
to a grief as old as the ages.

She was young,
        and very beautiful, as only
the young can be,
        but within such beauty
as bears calamity silently:

because it has run out of tears.

I closed the magazine and went
        outside to the woodpile
and split a couple of logs, thinking,
        "Her fire is likely
an open fire tonight,
        bright flames licking
and waving

like rising pennants in the breeze."

When I was a boy,
        I heard about the bloodshed
in Korea, about the Red Army

perched at our threshold,
        and the bombs
that would annihilate our world

forever.

I got under my desk with the rest of the foolish world.

In Okinawa, I wore the uniform
        and carried the weapon
until my eyes began to open,
        until I choked
on Marine Corps pride,
        until I came to realize
just how willfully I had been blind.

How much grief is a life?
        And what can be done unless
we stand among the missing, among the murdered,
        the orphaned,
our own armed children, and bear witness

with our eyes wide open?

When I was a child, frightened of the night
        and crying in my bed,
my father told me a poem or sang,

"Empty saddles in the o-l-d corral,
where do they r-i-d-e tonight."

Homer thought the dead arrived
        into a field of asphodels.
"Musashino," near Tokyo, means
        "Musashi's Plain,"
the warrior's way washed in blood.

The war-songs are sung
        to the same old marching measures—
oh, how we love to honor the dead.

A world without war? Who but a child or a fool
could imagine such a thing?

Corporate leaders go to school
        on Sun Tzu's *Art of War.*
"We all deplore it," the President says,
        issuing bombing orders,
"but God is on our side."

Which blood is Christian,
which Muslim, Jew, or Hindu?

The beautiful girl with the beautiful sad eyes
        watches, but
has not spoken. What can she

possibly say?
        She carries the burden of finding
another way.

In her eyes, the ruins, the fear,
the shoes that can't be filled, hands
that will never stroke her hair.

But listen. And you will hear her small, soft, plaintive voice
—it's already there within you—

a heartbeat, a whisper,
a promise broken—
if only you listen

with your eyes wide open.

America, Mon Amour

to Salah Al Hamdani, Sept. '03

The fascist in the White House can't hear,
can't see the faces of the suffering he authors,
nor can his brother, Saddam the Tyrant,
who remains in hiding, his finger still pulling a trigger.
All the little Caesars build their evil empires
of blood and castles made of sand. But empires
crumble, while the misery continues. Tyrants rise
and fall, and poets tell their stories.

In America, they've named a new poet laureate.
Caesars love their clowns, their little amusements.
But the poet from Baghdad continues in exile,
in Paris, and for twenty years couldn't call home
to his mother, and in Piacenza sings, "Baghdad, Mon Amour,"
and his voice never trembles. Even a little truth
can prove deadly. Nevertheless he'll one day
return to his home again, and the sweetness of his song,
more beautiful than silence, will lift me in its arms
because I will join him in Baghdad, mon amour,
because poets and people are brothers, sisters in the skin,
and because fascists can't live forever.

Salah Al Hamdani, your name and your song
are my prayer. It's true, blood flows like oil
and burns like oil, and it's the children who perish
for your tyrant and for mine. All the Caesars hunger
after money and power. All their empires
fall. Salah Al Hamdani, I invoke your name
and kiss your cheek here in Piazza Duomo

because the dead have no names in America,
the dead in Baghdad, the dead in Kabul.
The dead, the dead and the dying.
And those who merely survive.

Our Italian nights are full of wine and talk
and love. We have nothing but our songs
to stand against Caesar's throne and his call
for blood. Old men should fight the wars. But
it's always the innocent we send to annihilate
the innocent, filling their heads with lies.

The fascist in the White House sleeps well
most nights, guards at every door. Saddam is in
his castle or his cave, his guards guarding too.
The White House poet sleeps. Salah, what
can we tell them, what can we do to disturb these
sleeping giants? Italy is a world from ours, and ours
a world the Caesars and their jesters never knew.

Ma'assalama, Salah Al Hamdani. I invoke
your name to name the nameless, I invoke
your song to bring us all back home.

With Ilaria and Francesca in Piacenza

The years can be brutal—yesterday
a torrent, today just a drizzle. I sat
in the sidewalk café sipping cappuccino,
watching the morning's passersby. The girls
found me amusing, "like a grampa," they laughed,
"grizzled old poet against the war,"
who creaked down cobblestone streets in search
of ice cream or *granita,* a newspaper.

The girls I knew at such a tender age
wanted no part of me. And now my daughter
could, indeed, be their mother. They are beautiful
and intelligent, and happy to be kind
to the foreign visitor, practicing their English.
All of their joys and heartaches will rise
in time like summer storms, but today
they are laughing, teasing, laughing as only
girls can laugh, and the sun is burning off the clouds
as Plaza Duomo fills with noisy people.

Pigeons coo in the bell tower above the cage,
for sinners like me, that swings in the morning breeze.
I tell the girls, "I sentenced a couple of writers
to that cage last night, kvetching with friends
over pizza and wine at Pasquale's." Down here
in sweet samsara, the girls and I get a laugh,
and the cobblestones glisten and the air grows thick
and sweet as honey. *"Buon giorno,*
buon giorno," as happy people pass. Cappuccino

finished, I suggest a stroll and put on dark glasses
so Francesca and Ilaria won't notice
a tear in an old man's eye.

Arguing with Milosz in Vilnius

You are recently dead, old man,
    with your thunderous brows
and voice like a vast sea
    hinting at a dangerous undertow—
you are gone, your generation
    of testimony, of witness,
gone, gone among the ancient rites
    of passage, gone,
taking with you the innumerable
    names of the lost.

And yet I am here, walking
    the broad, freshly bricked avenue
of a democratic Vilnius,
    the Mother Sun
pouring amber on a world
    you would barely recognize,
where women are the ones
    dressed to kill, and the world
does what it will to be reborn.
    The poet is reborn
on each new old street,
    born in the process of the song.
You gave me Anna Swir.

Do you remember how we argued
    in Berkeley
when you told me, "I dislike nature,"
    and said it again
in comments on your beloved Jeffers—

"a huge museum of inherited images"—
and how could I not remember that
        as I rode in a van to Druskininkai?
How I loved the slender birches
        among the red pine,
the forest floor a bed of moss
        and a hundred kinds of mushrooms.
Bury a trout in mushrooms,
        cream and wine,
and bake it, and hear me sigh.

And you were with me again
        in "Scroundel Square"
(I renamed it) where the sculptures
        of the soviet regime
provide inherited imagery
        of another kind, museum
of our agonies and tragedies where
        I knew once again
that your world
        could not be mine—
and yet I am here, the bland faces
        and stern faces—Russian, Lithuanian—
of ordinary men who sold
        their countrymen for a song
are carved into my mind.

Tyranny is so banal.
        Jackdaws clack and squabble.
Sparrows flock to the square.
        Lenin Boulevard is gone.
I cross the square at the cathedral
        and turn up a narrow cobbled street,

15

Old Town, tiled roofs
    and freshly painted shutters,
where a hundred vendors will,
    in an hour or so,
present their wares to tourists.
    Four hundred thousand people
disappeared. Each had a name,
    a life filled with passion
and despair and all those
    ordinary irritations
too small and too many
    to enumerate—
It's more than one mind's heart can bear.

And yet the same brown river flows
    quietly between the same banks
as it did a thousand years ago.
    Here, it turns north.
Where is Bakszta Street? Where
    is Antokol? I sat
in the courtyard of the old monastery
    you so long ago admired,
the bench a little askew, grass overgrown,
    but a sanctuary from
the relentless noise of the city,
    as my friend Mindaugas explained
how you sought refuge here
    long before the war.
Was there a certain guilt
    from having merely survived?
Is it criminal to be lucky?

You were right, of course.
     "The struggle for poetry in the world
cannot take place in a museum."
     And the fact that you reject,
out of hand, my "eastern wisdom"
     also does not offend.
As little as I knew you, I knew
     you well enough to learn.
Our friend Rexroth introduced us
     on the streets of that great city
you came to call "nearly a home."
     You were a totem, an icon, a teacher.
Nevertheless, I say the world's a museum,
     the poem a record of survival
and betrayal, of human longing—
     vision and commitment—
and if I smell the bear or the wolf
     that once haunted the woods near here,
I say the wolf is alive
     in the eyes of men, alive
in the hearts of all who survive.

You were a great exile of the war;
     I was merely an orphan.
You were a child of Vilnius,
     of Europe; I was a child
of the wilderness of the west
     and know the track of the wolf,
the terrible odor of bear. Nevertheless,
     you civilized me some.
You were a great modernist,
     full of conviction,

sometimes a little short on patience.

I could not fully grasp your history
or your god. And yet I am here.

Vive la différence!

I bow to your presence
as I stand among the ancients.

On the Death of James Oscco Annamaría

When they found his body
in the trash pile
near Pachachaca Bridge
in Abancay,

no one could say
just who it was
who ripped the nails
from his fingertips,

who broke his legs,
who gouged out his eye,
who finally slit his throat.

No one could say
who dumped him in the trash
like a message in a bottle.

No one could say
who it was
or why.

But someone knows
whose hand is on the throttle
and whose is on the gun.

What did the young poet say
that he should have to die?
Were the authors of this tragedy
a death squad?

Trained by the CIA?
No one can say.

Someone knew the delicate
touch of his tongue
as it brought to life each
vowel and consonant of the poem.

Someone remembers
the tear in his eye
when he spoke of the death of Lorca,
the timbre of his voice
when he spoke of The People.

Someone remembers how he dreamed
of democratic music
in the shadows of the Andes,
of poetry with wings.

Surely, the young poet knew
that poetry is love,
and in this world,
love is a dangerous thing.

Canto Amor

To Martín Espada

*"For I am the sworn poet of every dauntless rebel,
the world over."*
—Walt Whitman

Inter arma silent leges, Martín.
They are subverting our Constitution.
They are at work everywhere,
building gulags and Guantánamos,
building empires in the sand,
destroying empires made of sand.

We are small among such mountains
as we listen for the voices
in the peasant chorus of the centuries.
But small as we are against war,
we defeat them with every song.

For we are rebel peasants of a kind,
listening with a peasant's
educated ear
for the social lie, for laws
that crumble under search and seizure
as the bodies are shunted away

into oblivion
at "Gitmo" —or anywhere
beyond the reach of law.

I thought of you today
while reading of the release

of Sister Carol Gilbert,
inmate 18056-
039 in Virginia,
and about her sisters in disarmament,

Sister Ardeth Platte
and Sister Jackie Hudson, the latter
from just down the road
in Bremerton.

These criminals—
of the Order Dominican—
offended the law not God's Law
by painting crosses in their own blood
on nuclear missile silos
somewhere on a slope in Colorado,

for which act Sister Carol Gilbert
mastered the art
of scrubbing toilets

in 33 months, and there
was privileged to meet Martha Stewart,
the American capitalist enterprise,
whose crime, apparently, was telling lies—

Oh, sweet irony
those old dead Greeks would love!
Two women behind bars, one
soft-spoken nun who wrote her truth in blood,
the other… a capitalist enterprise.

Pat Robertson,
Christian leader and former presidential hopeful,
today endorsed political assassination:
"It's billions cheaper than war."

Scales of justice sometimes swing.
I hear the laughter of Sophocles.
Poetry is an art
of listening.

I think of you, in your poem,
listening hard
for your grandmother's tongue,
long ago,
alone on a mountainside, or

you up late,
teaching Lao Tzu
or Bashō to your son.

One by one, the years
come,
but they fly like a cloud of crows.
My daughter just turned forty.

The struggle does not change: it's all
against the Law,
necessity rising from within:

Resist! Rebel!
Even against the laws of poetry
we must rebel.

And reaffirm. We stand
for the question, not the answer,
and dwell in the cave of Socrates.
Oh, don't you love it when they squirm?

When we put down the gun,
we placed our trust in the word, in the poem.
And that was the revolution,
the only one.

And God, I suppose,
looked down —
great black eyes of the white owl
in the bare winter birch
I saw through a broken window.

Everywhere
our friends are dying
of the same bloody question:
What *is* God's Law?
And what is ours?
And what is one life among billions?

Does meaning
have being?

Sister Carol Gilbert knows,
but does not kill for her conviction.
Esteban writes of militia,
Anwar of colonial war.

I am a monk with a begging bowl.

Three-fifths of one human being
demanded freedom long ago
and a thousand people trembled.
Ten thousand took up arms.

I was still a boy
when Emmett Till
was beaten dead
for putting a nickel
in a white woman's hand—

and his mother, my hero,
bristled, and said,
"Leave the casket open.
Let them see what they have done."

We are, yes, small among such mountains,
but we do listen—
for the voice of the peasant,
for the soul of the rebel—
we open the casket to see what we have done.

Somewhere in Baghdad's rubble,
some boy or girl struggles
to hear a different drummer, to see
not terror, but stars
trembling in the sky, imagining peace

and seeing the sun begin to set
across an opal sea.

He or she will marry the wind
and live somewhere
between apocalypse and heaven,

and the poem will be written
and walls will fall.

But our struggle will not end.

We must love our country, brother—
and therefore we must change it.
There is splendid fruit among the sour,
courage and beauty among the ruins.

Now's the time to celebrate being dangerous—
before they come for us.
Here's to a poets' revolution, to the joy
of being always on the side that loses.

Eulogy over, the casket open,
open the cask and pour the wine.

Here's to the mother of Emmett Till
who broke my heart and remade it; here's
to Rosa Parks and Sister Carol;
to all the old songs and singers who buoy us.

Come, singing Dionysus.

When there's bitter news from "Gitmo,"
I say,
sing "Guantánamera"
and set Guantánamo free.

And sing it again for me.

We will cultivate
the white rose in June, in January,
and be the deer that listens,
seeking refuge on the mountain,
wistful and hopeful,
dreaming an opal sea.

Vigilance

Trees, shrubs, grass—everything
        glistened in late February frost
as first rays of sunlight
        filtered through the woods.
I stood at the window,
        coffee mug in hand,
and watched the first spring robin
        hop and scratch and eat,

scratch, hop and eat, first under
        lace-leaf maples, then
along the edge of the path
        that leads out
to my studio. I watched,
        for almost an hour,
a happy bird enjoy a feast.

And for an hour, I put
        away all thoughts
of our president in Europe
        renewing threats,
put away all thoughts of
        people decimated
by a great tsunami,
        or of the latest casualties
in Iraq. The intrigues of
        little men with big ambitions.

Enough of that.
        Give me

one moment with a robin
and a sunrise,
late winter's harsh yellow light,
and crack
of frozen gravel underfoot
as I go out to work—
frightening off the bird—

a little wonder
in a suffering world,
a little delight
in a world of pain.
And then begin again.

TWO: LESSONS FROM THIEVES

Taos, 1958

Long ago and far away—
as the old storytellers say—

those long dusty roads rising
inevitably toward fabled plateaus
where a few frozen cows
and horses wandered in the sage,

winding canyons below ablaze
in the spreading sunset.
Huddled by our fire, my girl
and I read Rexroth and Lawrence

until the last noisy crow
brought nightfall on its wings,
then tequila and philosophy.
Our smoke rose in a plume

and disappeared. Our love,
our sadness. Her beautiful
country and its history. Her
slender body. Our desperation.

And our curse on the black heart
of Eagle Chief Carson.

Testament of the Thief

I always say the sweetest things
about those from whom I'm stealing—
I want them to like me, I want them feeling
downright comfortable in their skins.

I ripen them on platitudes—a kind
of psychological theft of sorts, it's true—
expressions of faux gratitude, good will—
while the left hand opens the till.

I never cause a disturbance—
no too-loud laughter, no angry glance.
Cautious, a bit withdrawn, but
friendly enough right from the start,

I leave behind the misery of my art.

Lessons from Thieves

1.

Someone has stolen my orchid—
nothing left but a circle
of emptiness in the dust.

Alas. Alas, goddammit.
I loved that flower too much.

2.

Was it the flower I loved,
or only the intricate
nurturing and the patience?

Winter solstice is over.
Soon the camellia will bloom.

3.

What you have taken from me
is merely your illusion.
What is mine cannot be yours

because you cannot grasp it—
no questions and no answers.

4.

Here is the Buddha's flower.
Is it his or is it yours?
The flower is your teacher

or your product, your emblem—
a dragon is in your fist.

5.
I'll cherish this emptiness
you left behind. "Attain *hsu*!"—
Lao Tzu—"Emptiness supreme."

The flower is in the pot.
The blossom is in the mind.

Nine Gates

1.
After reading the
twenty-fourth-or-fifth volume
of dull poetry
by the Most Acclaimed Poet,
I sighed and went out to pee.

A plump junco splashed
about in the bird bath and
somewhere a squirrel
complained at me bitterly.
And I felt oddly relieved.

2.
My aspirations
are all here. My poetry
will very likely
die with me, and that's okay.
It's just my way of getting

through another day,
of trying to be alive
as often as I
can be. I don't know the way.
I grope. I stumble. I fall.

It's all mystery.
For which I am most grateful.
Old fool that I am,
I'm happy in my skin. Shush!
Listen to the sparrow sing.

3.

Poetry is a
perfectly natural thing.
Some grows Sequoia-like,
taking forever to
become magisterial.

Some poems blossom
beautifully, only to fall
and be blown away
like cicada wings in the
pale, solemn dust of August.

A language is born,
a language dies. A culture,
a continent, or
a dream. Poetry is just
a moment when things appear

exactly as they
are—a rotting pear with bees
humming in nectar,
the exaltations of the
ever-industrial fly.

And you? And me? Don't
make me laugh. Our agonies
and our ecstasies
are no greater than a flea's.
What should one aspire to be?

The poem invents
its world— Bashō's frog captured
forever airborne,
frog and mind and foreknowledge,
in the moment before sound.

4.

"Look! There's Saigyō's moon!"
Chris Blasdel's shakuhachi
was also a moon,
a spotless mirror, playing "Sanya"
as the moon rose high over

Obakayama
in the spring sky. The *onsen*
faced down the valley,
tiered rice beds nearly planted,
their waters reflecting moons.

It was all a dream,
but I was there, lost in it,
those village faces
as they listened, lost in moons
over Nagano, carried

by each perfect note
as it bent, turned, or faded
into a silence.
What does it mean, Old Gaijin,
Big Fool on Big Fool Mountain,

this coincidence
or karma that makes moments
eternal? Tu Fu's
snow, T'ao Ch'ien's wine, Bashō's frog.
The ordinary. That's all.

Saigyō's whole bright moon
is a mirror reflecting

a world as it is:
a world of practice, a world
of this night being born.

5.

Before poetry
was called poetry, what was
its name? Before truth
was a word, there was still truth,
and it had a name. Shih-shuang,

writing long ago,
thought words were "expedient
means." Buddhas are born
of necessity. Shih-shuang
himself must have groped along.

6.

Each word carefully
tied to the next, the poem
is a net, and no
single knot is strong enough
to bear the burden alone.

Some nets are small, cast
for shrimp or herring. Some nets
are meant to hold whales.
In the ecology of
the poem, the fish is not

prey, but the surprise
catch of the day, a diamond
in the coal, a way
of awakening to something
just beyond what words can say.

7.

My wife sits in bed,
propped up with pillows, glasses
down her nose, working
crossword puzzles. It's Sunday
morning. She's feeling lazy.

She sips her coffee,
peers over her specs and says,
"Looks like a nice day."
I've been listening to cries
from Jerusalem, more cries

from Afghanistan,
and a president who cries
for war. But I say,
"Nice day," and make coffee and
go turn off the radio.

8.

If a poem is
a song, as some would assert,
its instrument is
the human voice. I listen
for the full or half-noted

vowel, for the crisp
measure of the consonant,
the modulations
that fascinated Denise.
Rexroth's seven syllables.

Creeley's compression
and vital tensions reveal
the real character
of the poem and the man.
It is in the line, measured,

whether in cadence—
Robert Duncan counting time
like a schoolmarm, hand
beating the triangle that
wasn't there—or the line is

otherwise composed,
it is composed by ear. No
other way to it,
but it rises, self-revealed
in the act of becoming.

Guy standing by me
at a Levertov reading

twenty years ago
whispers in my ear, "She reads
just like she talks. 'Cept her voice

seems to come from somewhere's else."

9.
A bodhisattva
takes a vow to wait at the
gates of Nirvana
until all sentient beings
become enlightened. That wait's

likely to be long.
Waiting for the poem, I
learn one small patience,
learn a way of waiting for
what arises from within.

Enlightenment is
beyond me. I struggle on.
May the poem bring
a little inner light
into a world of suffering.

May the poem sing
those weary blues again, or
let it speak of love:
it embodies what it is—
beyond what it is made of.

Enlightenment is
a path, not destination.
The poem's a gate,
a bridge, a haven. Enter
only at your own risk.

At the Japanese Exhibition

for Yusuke Keida
The elegant simplicity of Buddhist art.
Brocade kimonos and frothy tea.

The gaudy grandeur of Buddhist art.
Netsuke. Three-hundred-year-old bonsai.

Thousand-year-old duck eggs
like a mouthful of sulfur. Fresh cold sake.

Cold buckwheat noodles on a hot summer day—
with real wasabe. Earthen kiln-fired pottery.

A thousand ancient sorrows
behind a beatific smile.

The poignant beauty of butoh's grotesquerie.
Shakuhachi and feudal poverty.

Wabi-sabi. Sabi-shisa. Mono-no-aware.
Ukiyo-e masters who were almost thrown away.

A thousand delicate sorrows.

The Way of the Brush and The Way of Poetry.
Bashō's cricket, Bashō's cicada, Bashō's frog.

The Master's pure, clear word.
Issa's heartrending sigh.

Seven hundred years of blood
on Yoritomo's sword.

A Word in Farsi

My friend Farideh tells me
that in Farsi the word for poetry
is *sher*—from *shou-our,* she says,
which means *wisdom.* Poetry
is a blossoming branch of Igdrasil.

Sher and *shou-our* are the only words I know
in Farsi, and yet they are enough for now.
For how can one not love a language
from which poetry blossoms
from the wisdom at its root?

From the Chinese *shih,*
poetry is the word for *word*
married to the word for *temple,*
the temple a pictograph of the hand
reaching down, cradling a seedling.

Oh, how we abuse the temple
of the word, and oh, how easily
we resist the difficult music
of the wisdom at its root. But it's neither
as simple nor as difficult as we make it.

The wisdom of the poem
will, only later, fully blossom—
long after its roots, mere words
that are the temple's seedlings,
have been deeply planted.

Shih—sher—poésie—
that eternal translingual struggle
to embody the mantra,
to reveal not the answer,
but the mystery.

Sweeping the Garden

August dust settles
on all the tiger lilies,
bonsai larch and elm,
on maple and mugo pine:
dust of this world, dust of that.

Weeding the garden,
no dust mote on the mirror—
nothing to reflect.
The days begin to shorten.
Tonight the stars will be clear.

A Question Answered

What darkest night conceals, a sun exposes.
Yes, Joanne, there are evil men in this world.

We each have a little evil within us—
or else there is no good. Take myself: hardly
a model of Confucian rectitude,
I have stumbled along the dharma trail
like Old Blind Pew amidst a ship of thieves,
not knowing wing from tail, tap-tapping along
in his lust to find Nirvana. Perhaps
the sage is blind Tiresias, but I'm
no sage, just another fool among many,
one who has learned some things about pain.

There's loss and gain in almost everything.
"Do you believe there's evil in this world?"
Yes, I do. I have seen his smiling face,
his businesslike demeanor, his handshake.
I've gazed into his eyes in my own mirror.
We long in vain for some "essential good"
that is not within our reach. Buddhahood,
if it is attainable at all, comes
one step at a time, and along the way
the traveler comes to recognize
that there can be no darkness without light.

Solstice

Old snow turns to ice.
What solitary stillness
empties this cold world.

*

Snow-ladened cedars,
like monks in green and white robes,
all learning to bow.

*

One stick of incense,
one last bottle of sake—
one, and one, and one.

*

The moon, still alone.
Ten thousand whirling galaxies
and, simply, the moon.

THREE: MEASURED BY STONE

Gazing Down the Fairway, I Think of Po Chu-i

to Gary Lemons

I've thought of you often enough, old friend,
on the rolling fairways of Chevy Chase
during all those long years you didn't play.
Now old and gray, unable to walk the course,
I stand behind you again, recalling
the ancient Chinese sages who checked my
swing and kept my score the first ten years
I played. Golf is Zen. Throw the score card out
or keep it like a flower. Mulligans
are nourishment when forgiveness is required.

It's not about the score. It's not "about."
Not any more than Zen. Living masters
teach foolish men like us what playing means.
Zen begins in sitting and the back swing
is born in the mind. The swing is yogic,
the self most difficult to overcome.

Obi-One-Kabogy says our folly
is our wisdom: thinking too much, thinking
too little. It's simply the practice—all we
are in this moment, all we can become.

To Gray on Our Anniversary

I've relished years of bliss with you
despite the nefarious Hells
this suffering world has put us through.

I know you're not fond of growing old,
and what pain's to come, only time will tell.
Still, you are my comfort in the cold

of Odyssean storm-tossed seas,
my bride, my muse, my Penelope.

To Marvin Bell

The Dead Man balances a line on the turn of a phrase
      like Marvin Bell.
Balancing the line on the turning phrase,
      the Dead Man believes he is alive like Marvin Bell.
The things that escape his mouth embody the mind that is a mirror.
Mirroring the mind in its turning,
      the Dead Man turns a phrase
the way a cyclist turns the corner, shoulder leaning in
while the mind moves on beyond the turn,
into fields of estranged herons
      where Robert Bly, hair of porcelain and snow,
is listening to falling snow, and the Dead Man
spies the white horse's big round butt
      which is also white as snow
and reminds him of a kōan,
and the ghost of Williams slowly wipes his spectacles,
measuring each step in the snow, footsteps falling as surely
      as little poems with nothing to say,
and the Dead Man knows he too will fall one day
      as softly as this snow, as softly and rightly
as words fall into the open mouths of the hungry.

A Mountain

Denise's *Selected Poems* arrives
on a drizzly October day—
"The mountain comes and goes
on the horizon," she would say
with a girlish eternal glee. Or,
"Today the mountain / is cloud."

I first wrote to her almost
thirty-two years ago today,
from Surfboard Tech, the Channel Islands
bobbing in the waves. Now her book, *post
humus,* brings back her living voice to me.

Her laughter crackled
when she wrinkled her nose, squinted
and said of some old prize,
"He's really
not very good, is he?"
That laughter in her eyes.

Her pacifism, her courage.
Old compadre, old confidante,
old ally. And she giggled,
taking Gray's hand with a grand
conspiratorial twinkle,
about to tell a secret.

I didn't much like her god,
so we left Him out of it.
A walk in the Japanese Garden,

then a cup of tea by the lake—
religion enough for me.

Solitudes shared sometimes,
as when we mourned Abby's murder.

"We have only begun
to love the earth," and perhaps
begun too late.

There are poems to live with,
the life of poetry flowing
like a river, under
breathtaking maple,
in late October.

The mountain comes and goes.

In Memoriam, Nancy Foster

She was a wise old owl,
a patient watcher. I told her so,
and loved her for her laughter.
Thus I could not bring myself
to go and watch her die.
For what could I bring or do
but go and sit among her kin,
my family now, and watch
her daughters taking turns
beside her bed? I'd watch them
hold her hand and listen
as they whispered? She would never
have approved of that.

For she was a modest woman—
of modest ways and modest means—
who always asked, with a shy
conspiratorial smile, "Let's have
a little drink," reminding me,
"Remember to make mine
awfully weak." Still beautiful
in her last years, I'd watched
her gradually grow frail, seen
years of widow-sorrow
in those smiling tired eyes
that lit up quickly when we talked
politics or love. And oh, how we loved
to moan and cuss the born-again
gentry who would govern us.
We were happy unbelievers

together, and she was the mother
I never had in middle age—
nor for that matter, sooner.

When Gray called to say
it was finally over, I went out in the rain
and sat on the deck and drank
a bottle of bad *retsina* and smoked
a pack of cigarettes and wept
until I was soaked and numb
from grief and cold,
and then I went inside and played
some music Nancy liked.
I sat in the midnight dark with Miles
and Nancy at the table of my heart
until I almost laughed with happiness again
as I got up and went to bed,
because I knew she would approve
of my solitary wake.

Now the clan gathers.
Soon they'll deliver her ashes
to the family grave
a continent away.
May they make the least of it,
do it efficiently,
with kindliness,
with modesty, undaunted.

For that's how she would want it.

She cannot modestly protest
when I—modestly of course—

suggest we learn to carry
her spirit within us like a banner.

For that is the honor she bestowed on us.

To Quincy Troupe

I've only just heard
about your resignation.
You were probably
the best poet laureate
in this country's history.

You were the real thing,
the *poeta del pueblo*
Neruda called for,
bringing poetry and love
to "the people," as it were.

And who could resist
such charming intelligence—
joy, blues, compassion—
the naked jig of Williams
crying, "I AM a poet!"

Well, fuck'em, I say.
I'm not a "people's poet,"
so what do I know?
I live in my woods and work
for... for the good of the world.

Go back to Harlem
if you must. I know Harlem's
in your blood. Quincy,
my friend, the tide's going out
as the fog rolls in. The times

are treacherous. I,
a continent away, will
think of Harlem, stone
quiet Sunday morning as
you got out and I drove away.

The revolution
I care most about begins
only from within.
You carry it right along,
forgiving this world with a song.

To Doris Thurston on Her Eightieth Birthday

I hope that should I live to be
four score years or more,
I too will have learned to see
the beauty of this suffering world

through the eyes of a good-hearted woman.
What joy sustains and grief embraces—
the people, the stories, the places—
make it worth it to be human.

Bidding Farewell to a Friend

A harsh wind off the strait
after thirty-three days of rain.
Snuggled beside my wood stove,
I've enjoyed the company of many friends,
most of whom are long since dead.

Wang Wei stands at his brushwood gate
as Tu Fu sails down a snowy river
and Li Po pours more wine. Ms. Li
in her agony writes another elegy
to a tune that we've all sung.

What is friendship in poetry, after all,
but it sweetens the soul and
thickens one's skin? I don't know the answer
to the questions that go unasked.
But I've seen the face behind the mask.

When the bombs rained down on Babylon,
I turned to Salah Al Hamdani, fellow exile
still very much alive, and found
a brother sharing my contempt
for the vulgar suicide of war.

Tu Fu likes a man like that,
and I do too. But we are poets, and because
we are poets, we are failures—
and must learn to live with that.
Poetry, friendship, war—do ethics matter?

Those with whom I share a tongue
grow silent—only the patter of the rain
to break the silence of an afternoon,
to break the silence of an evening.
The ancient Chinese poet wrote

"Bidding Farewell to a Friend,"
to ask, "Will we ever meet again?"
I stand alone among the dancing trees
and listen to the wind. It blows in
from a sea that swells between us,

from mountains that divide.
I'll never see your island home,
nor learn about the palms, nor sip
your tea in the sun.
There'll be no stories over wine.

Your world could not be mine.
At the altar of the temple, I bow
to no one—*namaste*—
and go. But the sutra lingers on:
gate, gate... paragate...

The dust of this world is mine.
I'm going south of the sun
to celebrate with Esteban.

Awakening in Buenos Aires

What resplendent joy is found
in this February summer sun,
what nourishment
in the friendships of an afternoon!

I waken to the quiet of these city streets
that rang with laughter all night long.
It is a city that never sleeps.

Two cats doze atop a wall
between two gardens as the sun
breaks through a small marshmallow cloud.
Somewhere beyond where I can see,
a lone birds sings, high and sweet,
a welcome song a farther bird repeats.

Just off Jorge Luis Borges Street,
not far from Cortázar's little square,
I make a morning pot of coffee
from fresh-ground beans,
and greet the day and what it brings.

This city has awakened
from a century of stony sleep
in which the agonizing nightmares of the streets
were everyone's, awakened slowly
with a yawn to greet the flower
of the breaking dawn that comes
so slowly, but surely, comes

at last to lift a soul long lost in grief,
a soul that longs to sing.

The past is not past, but present
in our consciousness of where we've been
and what we've done—
that winding road without an end
that leads beyond the cemetery gates
into a world of breaking light, a world
of comradeship and ancient joys,
delights so old that even their mother tongues
are dead—and yet they live,
renewed in our renewal, made fresh
between two languages
perhaps only poetry can speak.

And those who disappeared, those who fell
into an unmarked dusty grave
or into the shining wine-dark sea
like Icarus in his melting wings?
They are you—and me—and everyone—
I've seen their mothers marching silently,
that they not be forgotten, that demons
never be appeased.
But they will never weep for me.

Bring me wine from Patagonia,
an empanada, and let me listen to
the sonorous gentle voice of Esteban
as it lights up a word or line
as brightly, warmly, as this summer sun.
Let me look into Patricia's lovely eyes again,

warm eyes that blaze with love and hope
kissing the cheek of husband, daughter, son,
or grandson on a lovely summer's eve.

All we ever really need is here, within us,
reflected in the poem or old song
I so poorly sing, the evening's conversations
slowly winding down, the warm embrace
that is not final, but is a promise,
a starting place, a glimpse of things to come.

It *is* as simple as that—
love, family, friendship, all honor
bound in alliance made
above a glass of wine, a bite to eat.

This is my prayer, for I have no god
but the silent one beneath the Bodhi tree,
who is no god at all,
but a friend to you, a friend to me.

Unabated, the world's wars drag on,
and what can any of us do but dream
of peace, and act accordingly,
and once again begin?
There's plenty of work to be done.

The history of our humankind is dark, cold,
wrought and writ in bloodshed,
grief and greed. And yet I weep
for joy—to have come so far
to find again what I believe:

how things—slowly,
but inevitably—can change,
and how our hearts
and this world can, at last, be made.

Strolling Calle Florida

Here it is Port Townsend, April,
and April rain. But my heart's mind
wanders, shining in the penetrating sunlight
of Calle Florida, in the bustling blare and glare
of that long pedestrian mall
about which every writer in the city
of good breezes has been compelled to write.

Calle Florida has flourished and darkened,
run red with blood, and flourished again,
nurturing writers, songsters, artisans,
and all their might-have-beens, poseurs
and hangers-on. Humility is learned
in the shadows of pretension. Here
is where García Lorca walked, and Neruda,
and didn't Storni meet her former lover
on that corner, fingering her gloves
while managing to be, almost, polite?

Here is the ghost of Borges, that old
Calle Florida bookshop habitué,
signing books in La Ciudad, sipping coffee,
holding court among the glitterati, now
cowering behind his *Obras Completas*
stacked against the stair, hands to ears
against the incessant invasive thrum
of hip-hop up and down the block.
How can a poet of shadow hold
a simple conversation in such clatter?

And don't I watch the very women
Riga watched—beautiful and inaccessible—
as they haunt a hundred shops
that peddle nothing I'll ever want?
And don't I hear the distant echo of
sonorous horse-and-carriage streets
Darío heard a hundred years ago?
All while I enjoy a latte and empanada
and a gypsy beggar plays his tango,
hat at feet, and tourists snap photos.

It is hard, Borges wrote, to believe
Buenos Aires had beginnings. But it did.
And history is written most often in blood.
This city was born the day Juan Díaz
de Solis, 1516 anno domini,
rowed up the muddy Rio Plate and met
the natives who devoured him.
And Spain grew rich while Spaniards
roasted and ate Spaniards on this riverbank.

The Italians came, the English, Germans,
Jews—each with their own Europe—
and made an almost European city—
the Paris of the southern hemisphere,
some say. But the architecture! What
a mish-mash of baroque, romantic, Franco-Italian
heresy, the clash of the modern, the stern
presence of German authority; neighborhoods
lined with acacia trees and green belts,
small parks and large, plazas shadowed
by ugly high-rise modern life... And all Chaos
somehow unaccountably beautiful to behold.

And because it is beautiful and its history
so often sad, I walk down Calle Florida
trying to imagine Borges' mother
calling masses to protest Juan Perón,
the poet's sister hauled off to a prison
"for whores" and spent a month there, sketching faces.
Or I walk the few blocks to the Plaza de Mayo
to walk in the steps of courageous mothers
who stand for those who disappeared,
who stand for social memory. Has Jacobo
Timmerman wandered an hour here?

Out of fierce darkness comes a light.
There is always a sadness in what is civilized.
Yet I think the city has a soul. The old haunts,
most imperiled already, cannot survive.
But democracy may thrive if the courage
of the poets is contagious, and if the myths
and legends do not conceal the real.
On Calle Florida, leather goods, fashion,
gypsy beggars, Che t-shirts and Big Macs.
What is the future of the past?

What can I know—a visitor, a pilgrim?
I gaze into the eyes of those who survived
decades of torment, grief, and anger,
and glimpse what I cannot ever know,
and am rewarded by the kindness of strangers.
The soul of the city is feminine, mature,
a mother who has loved and grieved—
whose grief defines her beauty

and her capacity for joy
as she welcomes one who loves her.

On the Third Anniversary of the Ongoing War in Iraq

a letter to Hayden Carruth

It's been nearly forty years
since you wrote that poem
about writing poems against
all those wars, Harlan County
to Italy and Spain. When your
Selected Poems arrived today,
it was one of the poems that
gave me pause reading it again.

We've been at war ever since.
I too, born in World War,
have lived and written against
that particular stupidity
and pointless, hopeless pain
all my agonizing days.
Has even a single life thereby
been saved? Who can say?
Except that doing so saved mine.

Oh, I could tell you about
saved lives. There was that
beautiful young woman in Sitka
whose husband, jealous
of her poetry, tied
her feet together with a rope
and threw her from his boat.
You have about 12 minutes of life
in those southeast Alaskan waters.

Or the grandmother in Utah
who wrote rhymed, romantic sonnets
and called me late one night
in my motel because her jaw
was broken, and her nose, and because
he was still drinking. Or
I could tell you about Alex,
doing life for murder over drugs,
and how his eyes lit up
when he discovered the classics.

Yes, poetry saves lives.
All wars begin at home
within the warring self.
No, our poems cannot stop
a war, not this nor any war,
but the one that rages from
within. Which is the first
and only step. It is
a sacred trust, a duty,
the poet's avocation.
We write the poetry we must.

Poem on His Sixty-third Birthday

It is heartbreaking to see
the cherry trees so laden with blossoms,
huge rhododendrons burdened
with swollen pink and red buds,
and lilies climbing hopefully toward the sky.

I did not choose to be born
in springtime, the briefest season.
But I may choose the day I die
if reason dictates such a choice be made.
Any day like this one would suffice.

See the bend in the cherry bough,
how pristinely white each blossom
hangs, holding tight, before the final fall.
The white stars of the new magnolia
have disappeared. The sun is burning

away the last faint trace of cloud.
I am certainly no Caesar, but have met
my Brutus and my Cassius in my day—
a knife in the groin, a knife in the face—
and delivered my poor man's empire

into the hands of fools and thieves
that only time will wash away. And I
have seen with weary eyes the resurrection
of the light, snows that always melt
into a dingy brown before the spring

returns to freshen a life again. Another
life. Again. Like Icarus, the lily
longs to meet the sky. And Icarus
himself must have blossomed in that moment
when his wings turned to honey.

We have flown and flowered, my love and I,
and have fallen too. But we are not,
as Borges thought, that river
of Heraclitus, time. Time is what it is
we so vainly try to cross, only to find

it and ourselves all changed, changed
utterly, although we are the same.
Mere flesh and bone, I step back into this one life
with eyes refreshed by a perishing world,
grateful only for this one moment, time

measured not by the flower but by stone.

Homeland Security

after Borges

No one is the homeland. The myths of history
cannot clothe the Emperor's nakedness,
no speech empower a vote not counted,
nor honor the living who are impoverished
by our anthems for the dead. No one
is the homeland. Not the heroes of our
old genocides, the Indian Wars, nor those
who sailed west with cargoes of human flesh
in chains, nor those in chains who came
against their will to work and breed and die
in the service of their masters, masters
whose sons would be masters of us all today.

There are no heroes except the ones
who rise to greet the dawn with empty hands
and heavy hearts in a brutal time. No oath
or pledge reveals what's in the heart or mind.
No one is the homeland. Or everyone.
For who lives without a country of the heart?
And yet we cry, "We!" We cry, "Them!"
I pledge allegiance to the kind.
Among the exiled, I make my stand.
No true democracy can be won
at the point of a loaded gun, nor honor found
in anthems or cheap paradigms
based on the social lie. No one is the homeland.

It can't be found in the grandiloquence
of pompous village idiots who run for office

because they want the power. Nor in the brilliance
of the medals on a uniform worn by a man
whose thinking is uniform and obedient
as he swears his pledge of allegiance.
The homeland is a state of grace, of peace,
a whole new world that patiently awaits.
The homeland is a state of mind, a light
flooding the garden, a transcendent moment
of compassionate awareness, one extraordinary line
in some old poem that reveals or exemplifies
a possibility... *in time... in time...*

Cairo Qasidah

A slow gray-yellow dawn
beyond the slow brown Nile,
a heavy haze over Cairo

as I stood in my window
remembering how we paused
on a bridge, Amal and I,
in fading evening light
last night
to watch a lean fisherman
and his beautiful wife
cast their net along
the stony shallows just
as they have done
for five thousand years,
their small son happy
astern, fingers trailing
in the water while Mamma
pulled the long slow oars
and Pappa drew up
emptiness again.

"Just wait!" they called to us.
And began again.

I rose in the hour before first light
having dreamt of them all
in troubled sleep all night—
a world caught

between antiquity
and modern life.
What kindness shone
in Amal's brown eyes
when she spoke of
her son, of her husband.
A little archeology
of the heart may be
sublime—or raise
a veil of tears.

Her smart young son is teased
when she declines
to wear the hijab. The rules
set against the erotic
create the erotic—the rules
of war are found
in a woman's hair.

The five o'clock call to prayer.
An infidel in every tongue,
I closed my window, turning
back to solitude again,
to sit alone and breathe.

Soon enough the streets
will snarl to life and the world
go about its brutal business.
What business have I
whose commerce is the gift
of words, mere poetry?
War and peace, love
and exile—a mother's love

or a poet's dreaming—

what words do we dare stand by?
For what good word
does the good soldier die?
What can any weary
traveler do but live
in wonderment and gratitude
amidst such poverty and splendor—

And I walked out into the dust
that veils the city,
enlivens the sunrise,
and will, soon enough, veil us.

To William Slater

I lie sweating happily
under the late October sun
beside the jacuzzi on the rooftop patio
of a rented flat in Palermo,
listening to the lovely Buenos Aires birds
that sing *Wa-weee, Wa-weee,*
from high in the branches
of stately old chestnut trees
providing shade for Oro Street
when November begins the months
of grueling summer heat.

Yesterday was *Día de Madre,*
and my wife, whom we both love,
each in his own way,
turned sixty. We strolled the afternoon
in the Japanese Garden
feeding over-fed koi
that rose from the deep,
then dinner with dear friends:
fruta del mar, good wine
and late talk in the cool evening breeze
of a favorite sidewalk café.
So exactly why was I so
utterly surprised
to find that I am still alive?

Wa-weee, Wa-weee, reminding me
of the Hanamaki "Buddha-bird"

in the mountains in north Japan
all those years ago, singing softly,
Bu-po-so, Bu-po-so.
Well, let them sing—those odd birds
and these—let all the birds
of all this suffering world
sing, and sing, and sing.
And find whatever song redeems.
They do not sing for you or me.

Today I read: six hundred thousand dead
in a dirty little President's
dirty little war
on the innocents of Iraq.
The sands shift, and we learn—
too often too late—that the heart
is the only gift we can make.

May this summer sun burn off
the sweat and tears I shed
when another, even smaller,
dirty little man
took what I'd made of years
with heart, tears, and callused hands.
I lay aside my book and wipe my brow.

We've grown too old for lamentations now.
I listen to the birds and rise
on wings of gratitude. I no longer read
the daily body count. The latitudes
of man's indecencies toward men
have long since fallen off the map.
The blues and oranges of your art

provide a welcome breath of air,
colors of the Buenos Aires countryside,
a freshening breeze.
Wa-weee, old friend, *Wa-weee...*

I have run out of elegies—
elegies for lost friends; elegies for
the unnamed, unnamable dead of war;
elegies for the animals, for whole
civilizations and so much more—
for the days, the centuries
that pass without regret.
What the heart plants, the heart begets.
Cruelty is good business, so it seems.

And yet a man alone can rise
to find transcendent joy,
as your art amply demonstrates.
What you have made and freely given,
Bill, cannot be destroyed
by little men who speak of love
and practice hate.
I could write a ream
on how you've shown me not to weep.

I rise and fold these old, arthritic legs
and gently close my eyes
and breathe.
And wait
for what each breath alone redeems.

SAM HAMILL is the author of fourteen volumes of
original poetry, has published three collections of essays
and two-dozen volumes translated from ancient Greek,
Latin, Estonian, Japanese, and Chinese. He is the
founding editor of Copper Canyon Press and the Director
of Poets Against War. His work has been translated into
more than a dozen languages.

Curbstone Press, Inc.
is a non-profit publishing house dedicated to multicultural literature
that reflects a commitment to social awareness and change, with an
emphasis on contemporary writing from Latino, Latin American,
and Vietnamese cultures.

Curbstone's mission focuses on publishing creative writers whose work
promotes human rights and intercultural understanding, and on
bringing these writers and the issues they illuminate into the
community. Curbstone builds bridges between its writers and the
public—from inner-city to rural areas, colleges to cultural centers,
children to adults, with a particular interest in underfunded public
schools. This involves enriching school curricula, reaching out to
underserved audiences by donating books and conducting readings
and educational programs, and promoting discussion in the media.
It is only through these combined efforts that literature can truly
make a difference.

Curbstone Press, like all non-profit presses, relies heavily on the
support of individuals, foundations, and government agencies to bring
you, the reader, works of literary merit and social significance that
would likely not find a place in profit-driven publishing channels, and
to bring these authors and their books into communities across
the country.

If you wish to become a supporter of a specific book—one that is
already published or one that is about to be published—your
contribution will support not only the book's publication but also its
continuation through reprints.

We invite you to support Curbstone's efforts to present the diverse
voices and views that make our culture richer. Tax-deductible
donations can be made to:
Curbstone Press, 321 Jackson Street, Willimantic, CT 06226
phone: (860) 423-5110   fax: (860) 423-9242
www.curbstone.org